nF421416

PRESSURE, HEAT AND TEMPERATURE

Physics for Kids – 5th Grade

Children's Physics Books

Speedy Publishing LLC

40 E. Main St. #1156

Newark, DE 19711

www.speedypublishing.com

Copyright 2017

Physics consists of many branches, including pressure, heat and temperature. While these terms may seem familiar to you, in the world of physics they are each unique in many ways that are not as evident as how we know them and understand them.

In this book, we are going to learn their definitions, how they are measured, and what happens when they interact with each other.

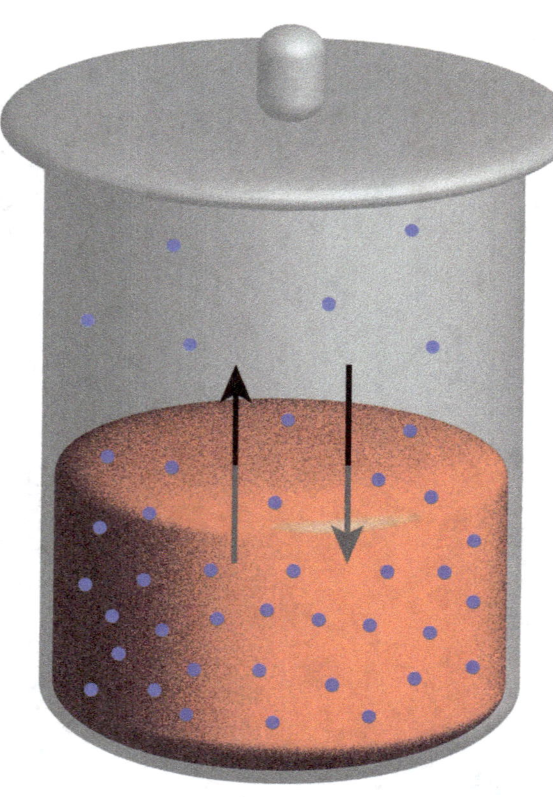

ILLUSTRATION OF VAPOR PRESSURE IN A POT WITH A LID ON IT

WHAT IS PRESSURE?

In the world of physics, the definition of pressure is the force placed over a particular area. When using similar force, the lesser the area of contact, the more pressure that is applied. The formula used in calculating it is provided here:

Pressure = Force ÷ Area or P = F/A

HOW DO WE MEASURE IT?

The basic unit of measure is the pascal, abbreviated as "Pa." Also, it is the newton per square meter as indicated in the above formula. Some of the other units used include the bar, pounds per square inch, otherwise known as psi, and standard atmosphere, or atm.

2
30
20
40
3
10
50
S
psi
bar
KI 1,6
4
0
MANOMETER

BLAISE PASCAL

The pascal was named after Blaise Pascal, a mathematician and French physicist. One pascal consists of a small amount of pressure. One atmosphere equals 101,325 pascals.

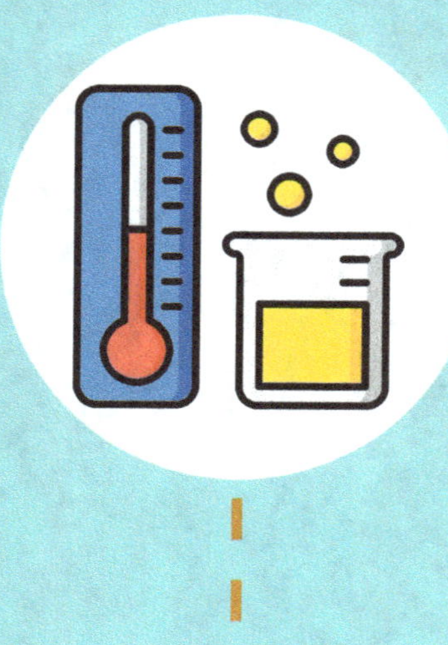

Examples:

If the block weighs in at 80 N and is lying on its side with area 2m by 4m, what would be the pressure used on the surface?

Pressure = Force ÷ Area

P = 80 N ÷ (2m x 4m)

P = 80 N ÷ (8m2)

P = 10 pascals

If the 80 N block now is on its end that is 2m x 0.5m, what is the resulting pressure?

Pressure = Force ÷ Area

P = 80 N ÷ (2m x 0.5m)

P = 80 N ÷ (1m2)

P = 80 pascals

BAROMETER ON A PUMP

ATMOSPHERIC OR AIR PRESSURE?

A significant type of pressure is pressure that is exerted onto an object from air, or Earth's atmosphere. Actually, this is the measurement of the gas weight above any object on a certain surface area. As the height of the elevation increases, the atmospheric pressure becomes lower and the air pressure is exerted since the object has less air pressing on it.

AIR PRESSURE

A barometer is a device used for measuring air pressure. Today's barometers measure it in millibars.

Changes in weather can be predicted by weather forecasters watching the changes of the air pressure.

If you have ever flown in an airplane, you may have noticed something going on in your ears, possibly a popping. This is caused by the change in air pressure.

METEOROLOGICAL INSTRUMENTS

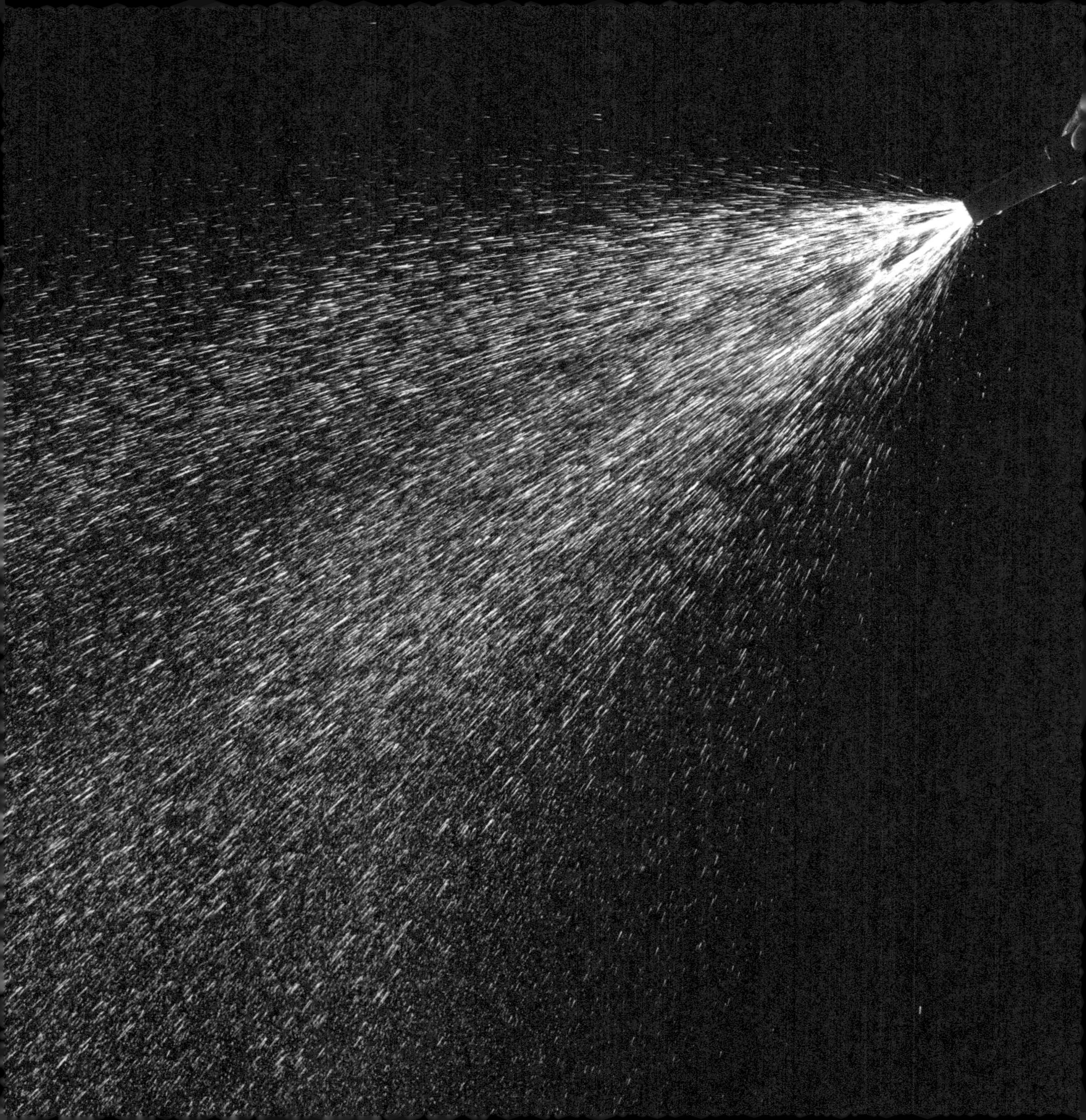

WHAT IS LIQUID PRESSURE?

Additionally, it is vital to find out pressure in a liquid or under water. The deeper you descend into the water; the pressure continues to increase. To calculate it under liquid, use the following equation:

$$\text{Pressure} = D * g * h$$

where D is the density of the fluid, g is standard gravity (9.8 m/s2), and h is the depth of the object.

A submarine has to be designed specifically to be able to withstand a very high pressure since they go very deep underwater.

SUBMARINE

Changes of States

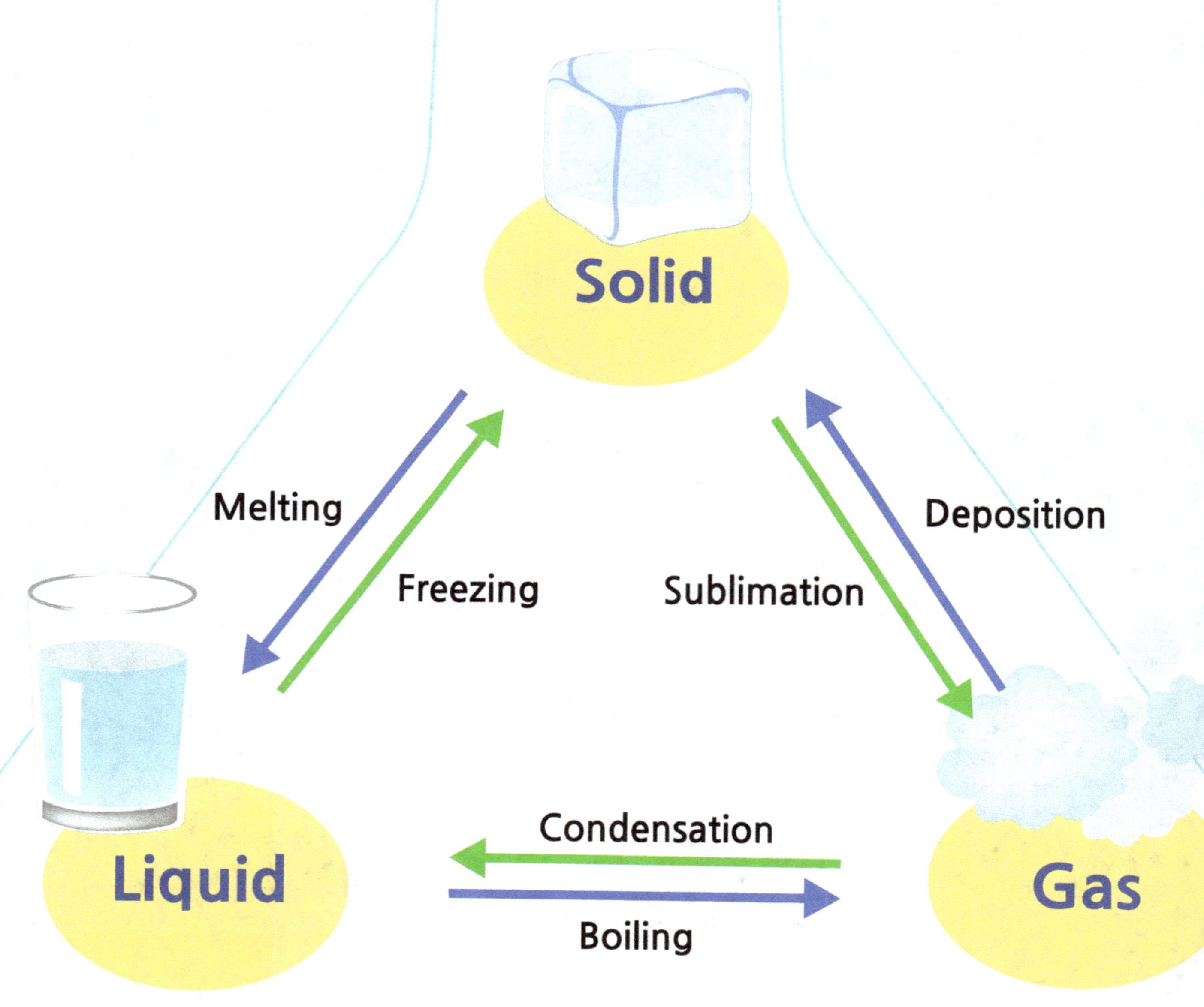

THE STATE OF MATTER

Pressure also impacts the state (or phase) of the matter. While we often think about states of matter as changing from a solid to a liquid, or a liquid to a gas, dependent upon the temperature, pressure also impacts the state of the matter. As seen in most cases, as pressure increases, a higher temperature is required to change the state.

The boiling point of water is a great example. When the pressure of the air is lower, as in higher elevations of the country, the water boils at a lower temperature.

250 ml
APPROX:
200
150
100
BEAKER WITH BOILING WATER

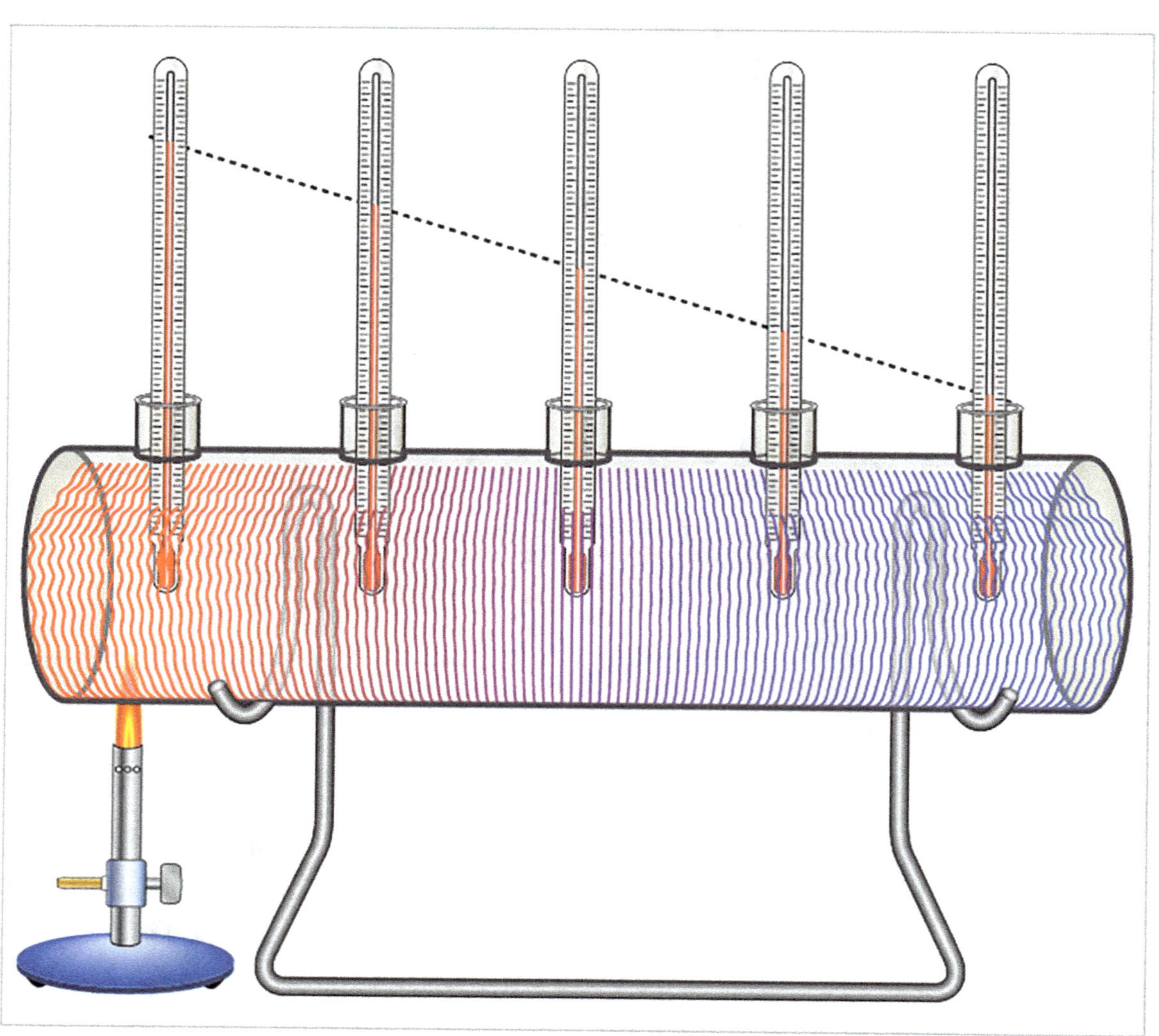

HEAT TRANSFER

WHAT IS HEAT?

The transference of energy from one object to another object because of the temperature difference is known as heat. It is measured in calories, joules or BTUs (British Thermal Units).

While temperature and heat are related closely, they are not considered to be the same. An object's temperature is determined by how quickly its molecules are able to move. The faster they are moving, the higher the temperature. We know objects having a high temperature as hot, and objects that have a low temperature as cold. Sound familiar?

HOT
COLD

THE METAL CONDUCTS HEAT FROM THE CUP OF HOT WATER TO THE CUP OF COOL WATER AND VISE VERSE

HEAT TRANSFERENCE

As two objects touch each other, or are combined, their molecules transfer energy that is referred to as heat. They will attempt to get to the point where their temperature is the same. This is referred to as equilibrium. The heat flows from the hot object to the cold one. The hotter object's molecules slow down and the colder object's molecules speed up.

They eventually will get to the same temperature.

This process occurs around you all of the time. Think about it, if you take a cube of ice and place it in a soda that is warm, the ice cube melts and the soda cools down.

HOT COFFEE

A GIRL DRINKING COLD SODA

EXPANSION OF HOT OBJECTS

As something gets hotter, it gets bigger, or expands. Similarly, as an item gets colder, it shrinks. This is how mercury thermometers are made. Liquid mercury is used for the line of the thermometer.

As it gets hotter, it expands and rises to indicate the temperature. The expansion and contraction resulting from the temperature allows the thermometer to work.

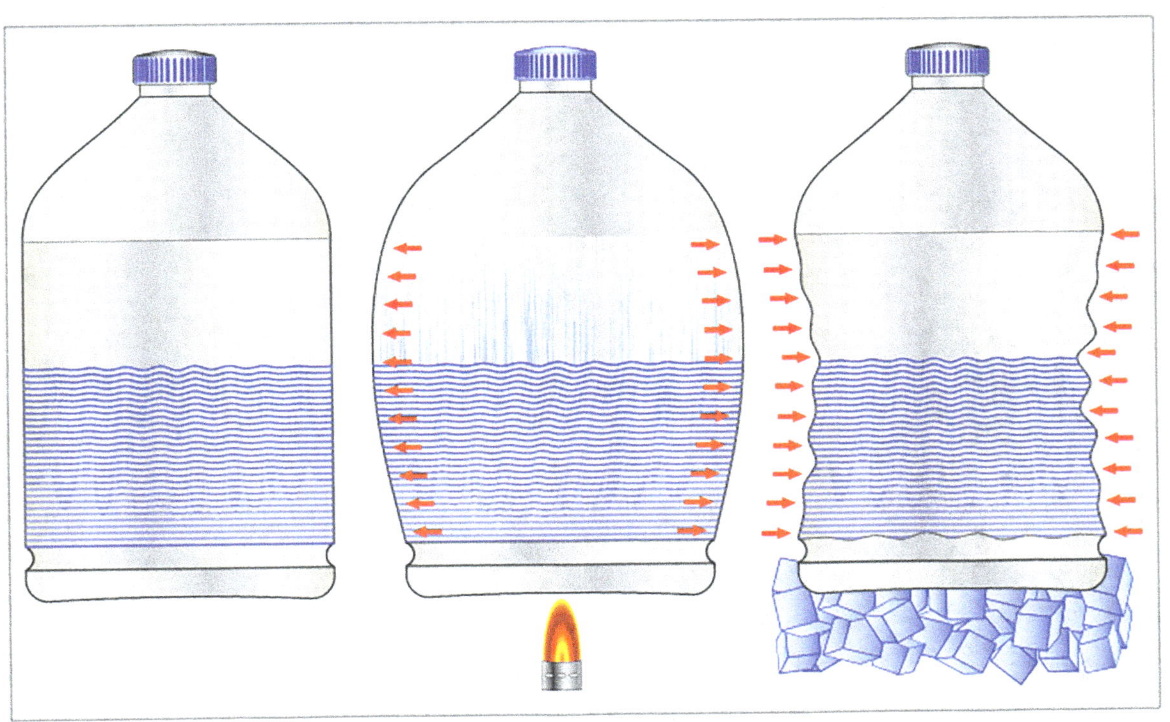

GAS PRESSURE

BOILING POT OF LIQUID

CONDUCTION

As heat is transferred from one item to another one, this is known as conduction. There are some materials that are able to conduct heat better than other ones. For example, metal is a good heat conductor.

Metal is used in pots and pans for cooking since it moves the heat from the burner to the food rapidly. On the other hand a blanket, being a cloth, is not a good heat conductor. Since it is not a good heat conductor, it works great at keeping us warm since it won't conduct (remove) our body heat to the cold.

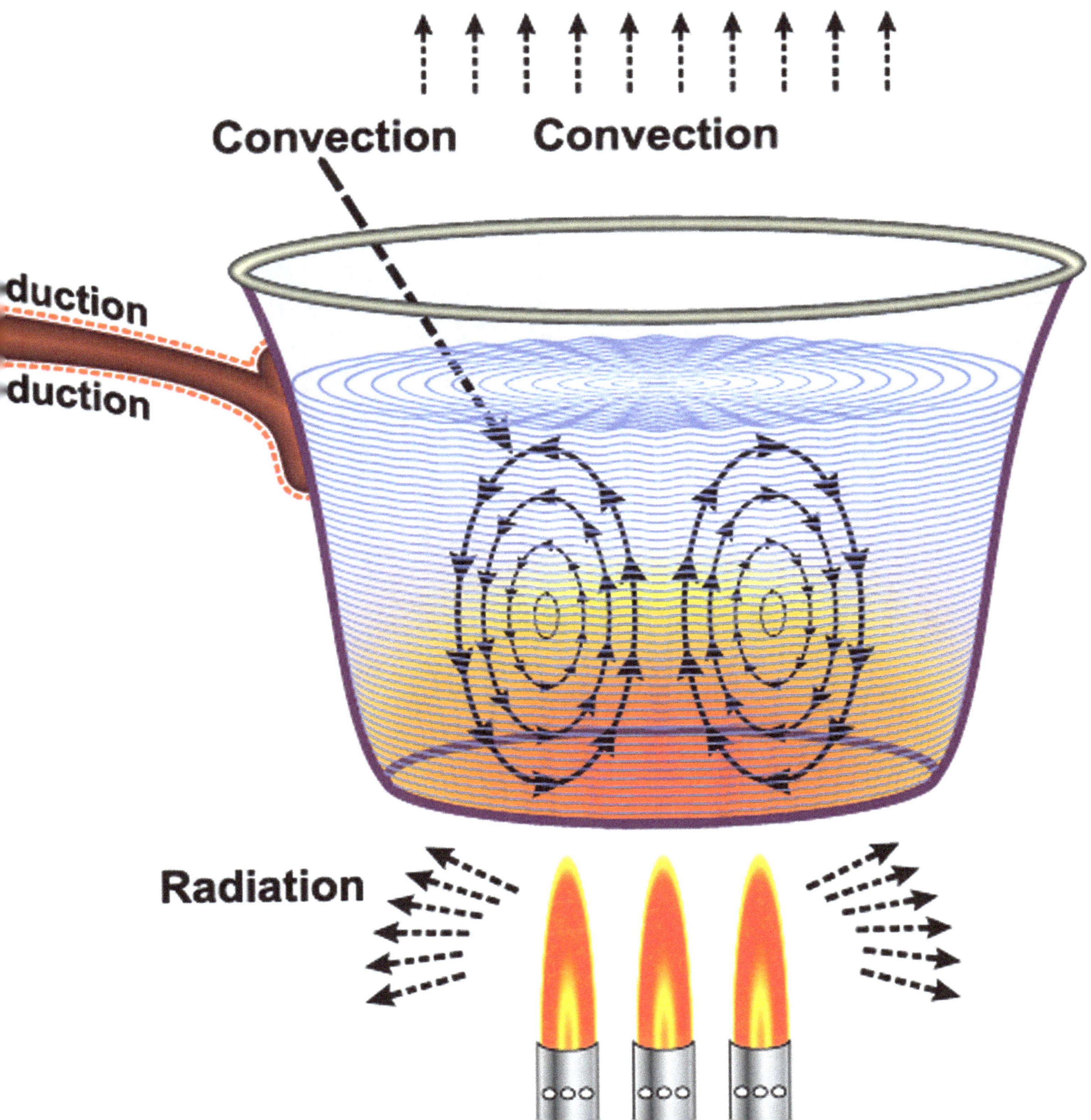

Convection
Convection
duction
duction
Radiation

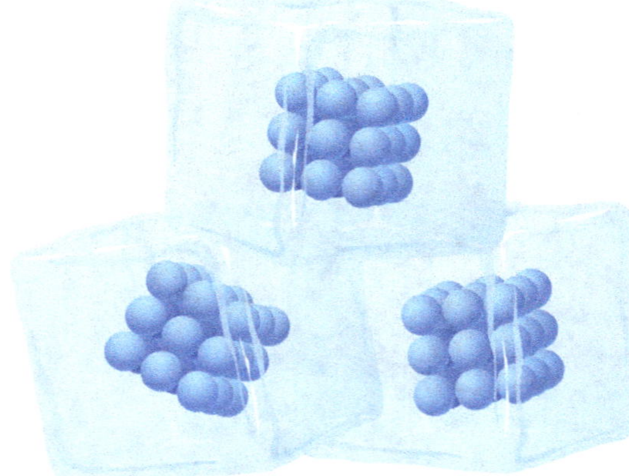
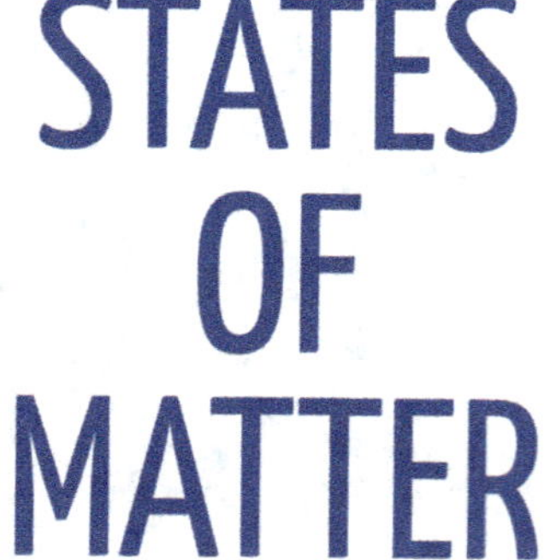
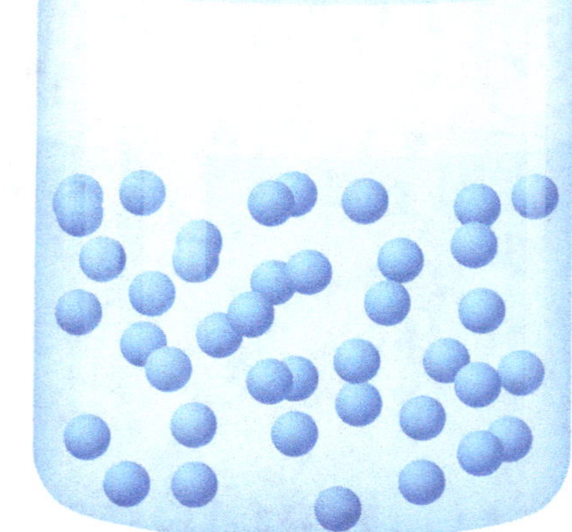

SUBLIMATION
DEPOSITION
CONDENSATION
EVAPORATION
STATES
OF
MATTER
MELTING
FREEZING

STATES OF MATTER

Heat impacts the state of matter. Based on temperature or heat, the state of the matter can be changed. Gas, liquid, and solids are the three states that matter can take on dependent upon the temperature.

An example is when water is cold, and its molecules move very slowly, it becomes ice (solid). As it become warmer, the ice melts and the water then becomes a liquid. If you then add more heat to the water (i.e. boiling), the molecules begin moving quite fast and it then becomes steam (gas).

COLD WATER WITH ICE

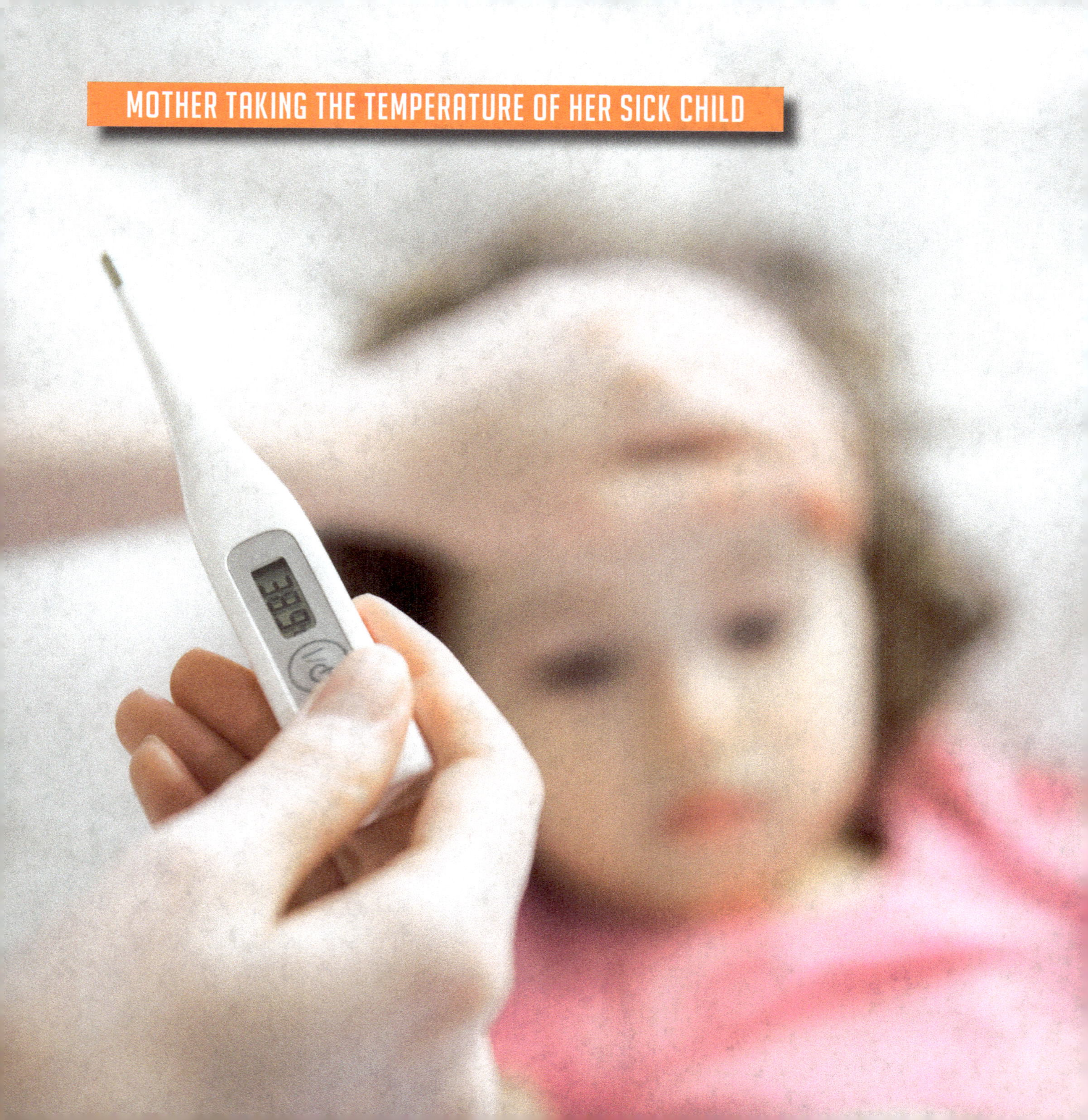

MOTHER TAKING THE TEMPERATURE OF HER SICK CHILD

TEMPERATURE

Believe it or not, temperature is difficult to define as a property. While we use it in our ordinary lives when describing the coldness or hotness of something, in the world of physics, the definition is the average kinetic energy of moving particles in a substance.

THERMOMETERS

Thermometers utilize a scientific property known as thermal expansion. As the temperature of a substance increases, most will expand and take up additional volume.

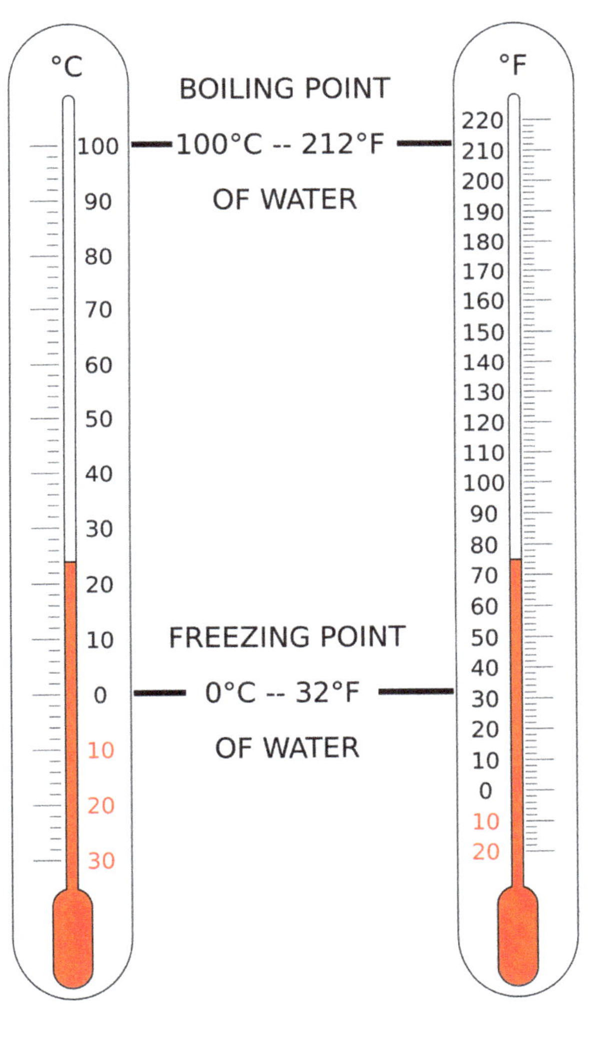

°C
°F
BOILING POINT
100°C -- 212°F
OF WATER
100
90
80
70
60
50
40
30
20
10
0
10
20
30
220
210
200
190
180
170
160
150
140
130
120
110
100
90
80
70
60
50
40
30
20
10
0
10
20
FREEZING POINT
0°C -- 32°F
OF WATER
CELSIUS
FAHRENHEIT

80 mL
± 5%
60
40
20
BEAKER AND FLASK WITH BLUE WATER AND
THERMOMETER IN SCIENCE LABORATORY

Liquid thermometers use some type of substance (mercury was used in the past, but alcohol is typically used today) enclosed is a small, glass tube. When the temperature increases, the liquid expands to fill up more of this tube. As the temperature decreases, the liquid then contracts and takes up a less amount of the tube.

HOW DO WE MEASURE TEMPERATURE?

A thermometer is used to measure it. There are various standards and scales that are used including Kelvin, Fahrenheit and Celsius.

Celsius is the most commonly used scale around the world. It is abbreviated as °C and its unit is "degrees". This scale sets water's freezing point at 0 °C and water's boiling point at 100 °C.

COUPLE FANNING THEMSELVES TO COOL DOWN

°C
°F
50
F
120
100
80
THERMOMETER

Celsius was named for Anders Celsius, a Swedish astronomer. Originally, Celsius was known as "centigrade."

Fahrenheit is the most commonly used scale in the United States. It is abbreviated as °F and set water's freezing point at 32 °F and water's boiling point at 212 °F. This scale was named after Daniel Fahrenheit, a Dutch physicist.

Kelvin is the unit most used by scientists. It does not use a ° symbol. To write a temperature in Kelvin you simply use the letter K. Absolute zero is the 0 point of its scale. It uses increments similar to Celsius, 100 increments between water's freezing and boiling points. This scale was named for William Lord Kelvin, who was born in Belfast, and was an engineer and physicist.

THE WOMAN SET'S THE DESIRED TEMPERATURE IN HOME HEATING SYSTEM

WILLIAM LORD KELVIN

CONVERTING SCALES

Celsius and Fahrenheit °C = (°F - 32)/1.8 °F = 1.8 * °C + 32°

Celsius and Kelvin K = °C + 273.15 °C = K - 273.15°

Absolute Zero

The coldest possible temperature which any substance can achieve is known as absolute zero. It equals 0 Kelvin or -273.15 °C (-459.67°F). The average temperature of today's universe is about 2.73 kelvins, or -270.42 degrees Celsius; -454.76 degrees Fahrenheit.

There are so many more branches of physics to learn about. For additional information about heat, pressure, and temperature or any of the other branches of physics, you can go to your local library, research the internet, and ask questions of your teachers, family, and friends.

Visit

BABY PROFESSOR
EDUCATION KIDS

www.BabyProfessorBooks.com

to download Free Baby Professor eBooks and view
our catalog of new and exciting Children's Books